Genes

D1149223

f

Genesis to Jesus

Making sense of the Old Testament

Dave Burke

frameworks

FRAMEWORKS
38 De Montfort Street, Leicester LE1 7GP, England

Unless otherwise stated, Scripture quotations in this publication
are from the Holy Bible, New International Version. Copyright ©
1973, 1978, 1984 International Bible Society. Published in Great
Britain by Hodder & Stoughton Ltd.

First published 1991

British Library Cataloguing in Publication Data
Burke, Dave
   Genesis to Jesus.
   1. Christianity. Scriptures   2. Bible. O.T.
   I. Title
   221

ISBN 0–85111–219–6

Set in 10½ on 12½ Palatino

Typeset in Great Britain by Intype, London
Printed and bound in Great Britain by
Cox & Wyman Ltd, Reading

*Frameworks is an imprint of Inter-Varsity Press, the book-publishing
division of the Universities and Colleges Christian Fellowship.*

Contents

List of Maps and Diagrams

Foreword

*T*HIS is a sketch of the flow of events from the dawn of time to the appearance of Jesus Christ as described in the Old Testament. Like a sketch map it picks out some details at the expense of others. But the purpose is to help newcomers to find their way around the first three-quarters of the Bible and to introduce the main landmarks. Scholars may scoff at its skimpiness, but then it is not intended for them, they need more detailed charts to guide them.

My own exploration has been helped and inspired by a number of people over the years. I'm grateful for the scholarship of Paul Laurence who helped me get so many Old Testament facts straight when we worked together on an audio-visual script about Old Testament history. I'm grateful too for the insights of Dr David Gooding and his willingness to share them. Both of these people have influenced this book significantly, though any errors you may find here are not theirs but mine!

Special thanks go to Linda Fox and Val Wells who typed up this book during its gradual evolution. Thanks also to Charles Read for his help with the section 'What the books are about'.

Dave Burke
Leicester, 1991

Introduction

*I*T was evening, and as two disciples walked to Emmaus, they were joined by a stranger. They did not recognize that he was the newly risen Jesus. As the three walked, their conversation turned to the Old Testament writings.

The 'stranger' did most of the talking: 'And beginning with Moses and all the Prophets, he explained to them what was said in all the Scriptures concerning himself' (Luke 24:27).

Jesus was able to point to himself at many places in the Old Testament. It would be interesting to know what he said!

Their journey was seven miles long, a maximum of three hours walking, even at a very slow pace. Jesus covered a lot of ground in a very short time . . . and so will we!

Paul's second letter to Timothy is full of advice about how to live a Christian life that really counts. As Paul wrote, he urged Timothy to study his Old Testament: 'All Scripture is God-breathed and is useful for teaching, rebuking, correcting and training in righteousness, so that the man of God may be thoroughly equipped for every good work' (2 Timothy 3:16–17).

The Old Testament is a handbook for effective Christian living . . . indeed the first Christians didn't have a New Testament at all. Yet many Christians remain very ignorant of what is going on in the Old Testament. Why is this?

Perhaps it is something to do with the Old Testament's complexity; the books are not in chronological order but grouped together in 'styles'. The Old Testament as a whole is a huge book and requires great effort to master it. Then it is often boring. Great, long pagefuls of barely understandable laws or poetry, or worse – lists of names! And it is all very removed from us – too ancient, too distant, too irrelevant for this modern bustling world.

Well, that's how it seems anyway, yet Jesus thought the Old Testament was relevant, and Paul thought it was essential – by the time you have read this short book perhaps you will too!

CHAPTER 1

············

Creation and Fall

▬▬▬▬

*T*HE Old Testament begins with the majestic declaration that the universe is not an accident, but a deliberate act of creation by an all-mighty being: 'In the beginning God created the heavens and the earth' (Genesis 1:1).

The crown of this creation is humankind.

> *Then God said, 'Let us make man in our image, in our likeness, and let them rule over the fish of the sea and the birds of the air, over the livestock, over all the earth, and over all the creatures that move along the ground' (Genesis 1:26).*

Rulers of the earth

Man and woman are proclaimed rulers of the earth, God's 'vice regents', bearing the moral, spiritual and creative image of God; perfectly reflecting his purity and holiness. So Genesis' description of the primeval world puts human beings at the centre of the creation.

The results of several centuries of industrial development have made modern Christians a bit embarrassed about this. Some environmentalists blame this creation-mandate to rule the world for humanity's arrogant misuse of planet Earth. Yet the first people were told to 'take care of' the earth (see Genesis 2:15), not plunder it. We were meant to tend the planet carefully, as though looking after it for someone else. Genesis tells us that something terrible happened in our early history that led to our treating the earth as though we owned it.

Humanity was made with the ability to make choices — free, but not robots. We could choose to obey or disobey God. Genesis describes how Adam chose independence and disobedience – choosing to stand alone.

To the average twentieth-century person the idea of facing the challenge of the universe alone is a noble and beautiful thought, but to the biblical writers it was a sordid tragedy; humanity became a spiritual corpse. Our disobedience led to a total breakdown of what God had created for garden Earth. So, in Genesis 3, God passes sentence: Man and woman are exiled from the garden and alienated from God's presence. We are even alienated from each other and the beautiful world we were intended to inhabit.

We now live in a fallen world. God is a distant and unapproachable being for the majority of humankind. So we have problems knowing what is the meaning of our existence, and even in deciding how we should behave towards one another. Man and woman have become enemies, and we still struggle to resolve the conflicts between us. Humanity and nature have become enemies, and the world we were meant to occupy as tenants we now treat as our own.

Our environment, as well as our relationships with each other, bear the scars of our rebellion against God. The second sin in the Bible is a murder. As earth's primeval history gets under way, the fruit of our moral failure and spiritual blindness is a society that God begins to regret having created.

The flood

> The LORD saw how great man's wickedness on the earth had become, and that every inclination of the thoughts of his heart was only evil all the time. The LORD was grieved that he had made man on the earth, and his heart was filled with pain. So the LORD said, 'I will wipe mankind, whom I have created, off from the face of the earth – men and animals, and creatures that move along the ground, and birds of the air – for I am grieved that I have made them.' But Noah found favour in the eyes of the LORD (Genesis 6:5–8).

God flooded the earth and flushed it clean of its evil population; but he withheld from total annihilation. Noah and his family escaped by obeying God and building a lifeboat.

The flood eventually subsided and Noah resettled his family on the devastated earth, their descendants spilling around the world with the command to fill it. 'As for you, be fruitful and increase in number; multiply on the earth and increase upon it' (Genesis 9:17).

God's judgment had *purified* the earth, but it hadn't *solved* the problem of sin. This was to become rapidly apparent as these descendants of Noah expanded into the Euphrates valley.

> Now the whole world had one language and a common speech. As men moved eastward, they found a plain in Shinar and settled there.
> They said to each other, 'Come, let's make bricks and bake them thoroughly.' They used brick instead

of stone, and bitumen for mortar. They said, 'Come, let us build ourselves a city, with a tower that reaches to the heavens, so that we may make a name for ourselves and not be scattered over the face of the whole earth.'

But the LORD came down to see the city and the tower that the men were building. The LORD said, 'If as one people speaking the same language they have begun to do this, then nothing they plan to do will be impossible for them. Come, let us go down and confuse their language so they will not understand each other' (Genesis 1:1–7).

As these early builders laid the foundation of what some scholars believe to be the city of Babylon, God frustrated their plans and forced them to stop.

Putting it together

Here in Genesis you have two different stories of judgment. What are they really about?

1. The flood is a 'prototype' – a model or illustration of the way that God has chosen to work in history. It tells us two things:

Firstly, his intention to judge is immovable and certain. We know that God *will* judge humankind because he has already done it once. And he will do it again. This is why, so often, people hate the story of the flood.

Secondly, he will always choose to save some. Not because they deserve it but just because of his love for us. People say, 'How can God send people to hell?' But a better question is, 'Why does he choose to save anyone at all?'

2. Babel or Babylon is a symbol in Scripture – you will meet it again and again in the prophetic books of the Old and New Testaments. It symbolizes sheer human pride in all its ugliness. H. L. Ellison writes, 'For Isaiah, Babylon was not merely a city on the Euphrates, but it was a symbol of human society when it rises up against God and his will.'[1]

In a society like ours we need to listen to the message of Babel. The modern world has pushed God out of the centre of our lives. Personal and national decisions are made without reference to him or his Word, the Bible. He is very patient but will not allow himself to be ignored or marginalized for very long.

The story of Babel reminds us that his judgment is real and terrible even when it does not involve total destruction!

The early chapters of the Bible's history are full of failure and judgment. Yet they also reassure us that God is not prepared to let all humankind go to ruin. At the very beginning he promised a rescuer to men and women in the sentence passed on the serpent:

> So the LORD God said to the serpent, 'Because you have done this,
>
> > 'Cursed are you above all the livestock
> >   and all the wild animals!
> > You will crawl on your belly
> >   and you will eat dust
> >   all the days of your life.
> > And I will put enmity
> >   between you and the woman,
> >   and between your offspring and hers;
> > he will crush your head,
> >   and you will strike his heel'
> >   (Genesis 3:14–15).

This early promise is very vague but it will begin to make sense as the Old Testament story unfolds.

Notes

1. H. E. Ellison, *The Message of the Old Testament* (Paternoster Press, 1969).

CHAPTER 2

....

The Patriarchs – God's Promise Gets Under Way

─────────

*A*BOUT four thousand years ago a prosperous business man lived in a city called Ur of the Chaldees, on the banks of the Euphrates. His name was Terah and his city was the jewel of the ancient Middle East, the capital of the world's most advanced and sophisticated civilization.

Terah took his whole family and set out from Ur to travel to Canaan, following the long caravan route northwards to avoid crossing the inhospitable desert. Yet this affluent Chaldean merchant never reached his destination, choosing instead to settle at the half-way point in a city called Haran. There, God spoke to Terah's son who was known as Abram:

> The LORD had said to Abram, 'Leave your country, your people and your father's household and go to the land I will show you.
>
> > 'I will make you into a great nation
> > and I will bless you;
> > I will make your name great,

and you will be a blessing.
I will bless those who bless you
*   and whoever curses you I will curse;*
and all peoples on earth
*   will be blessed through you.'*

So Abram left as the LORD had told him. . . Abram was seventy-five years old when he set out from Haran (Genesis 12:1–4).

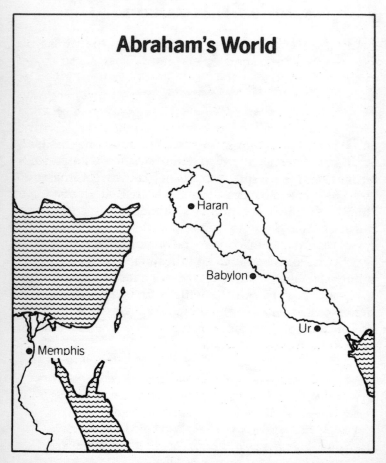

To underline the fact that his life was now under new management, God changed Abram's name. From then on he was called *Abraham*. In the last chapter we looked at prototypes (Noah's flood) and symbols (Babel), and we saw that these appear quite frequently in the Old Testament. If there was ever a prototype of the normal Christian life it is Abraham!

The example of Abraham

Firstly, he was called from an unbelieving pagan city to live the life of a nomad for the Lord. That is the model of the Christian life that the New Testament gives us (read Hebrews 11:8–10). Secondly, he was given a promise which was never fulfilled in his lifetime (read Hebrews 11:11–12) though it became reality later. Thirdly, and ironically, although he became famous for his faith in God (and was even prepared to sacrifice his own son), he was not always so impressive (compare Genesis 20 with 22). His faith grew as God tried and tested it. Finally, and most wonderfully, his embryonic faith was enough to save him! (See Genesis 15:6 and Romans 4:1–2.)

For centuries, Christians have found the ups and downs of Abraham's life uncannily like their own wobbly walk with God! That's why his story is such a challenge and encouragement to us today. Read it in Genesis! Abraham's nomadic lifestyle was continued by his son Isaac and grandson Jacob. God repeated a familiar promise to each generation:

> 'I will give you and your descendants the land on which you are lying. Your descendants will be like the dust of the earth, and you will spread out to the west and to the east, to the north and to the south. All peoples on earth will be blessed through you and your offspring' (Genesis 28:13b–14).

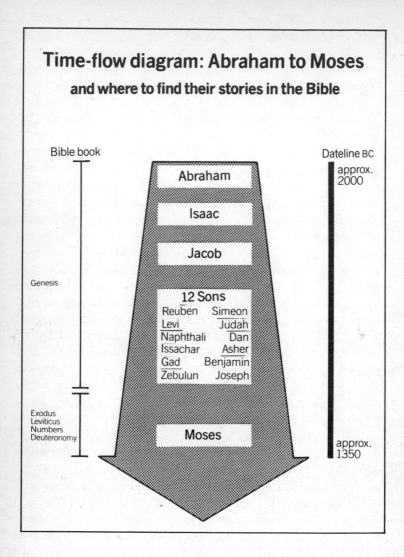

Time-flow diagram: Abraham to Moses
and where to find their stories in the Bible

Bible book

Dateline BC

approx.
2000

Abraham

Isaac

Jacob

Genesis

12 Sons

Reuben	Simeon
Levi	Judah
Naphthali	Dan
Issachar	Asher
Gad	Benjamin
Zebulun	Joseph

Exodus
Leviticus
Numbers
Deuteronomy

Moses

approx.
1350

How would he bless the whole world through a descendant of Abraham? Time will tell!

Joseph – a rags-to-riches story

God renamed Jacob, *Israel*, and in time he had twelve sons: *Reuben, Simeon, Judah, Dan, Naphthali, Gad, Asher, Issachar, Zebulun, Levi, Joseph* and *Benjamin*. Ten of these gave their names to ten of the twelve tribes of Israel. All except Joseph and Levi: Joseph's two sons, Manasseh and Ephraim gave their names to the other two tribes. Levi became a tribe of priests without an official piece of the promised land to inherit, the other tribes were required to look after their material needs.

Joseph inspired the jealousy of his older brothers and they hatched a plot to sell him into slavery. He found his way to Egypt and eventually to a position of great administrative importance. This rags-to-riches story looks like a fairy tale. However, Joseph entered Egypt during a period of intense foreign immigration. (This is well attested by archaeology.) At first these foreigners took up mundane bureaucratic jobs but later became far more senior in their positions. Against this background the story of Joseph is quite believable and you can read it in Genesis 37–50.

During a famine Joseph was put in charge of food distribution and in time his hungry brothers emigrated to Egypt to find food. Joseph then arranged for his whole family to emigrate and live in the fertile area of Goshen in the Eastern Nile delta.

Life on fallen earth is a risky business. Even a servant of God can be victim of apparent disaster, like being sold into slavery! Joseph and his brothers demonstrate the truth of the New Testament principle that 'all things work together for good' (Romans 8:28) for the people of God. Their temporary misfortune led to their salvation, and that means our own setbacks can be key influences in making us into the kind of people God wants us to be. Looking back, the bad times can be the best times!

Life in Egypt was quite attractive. Yet the cream of Egyptian society lived off the backs of a massive army of slaves. After Joseph's death, they became wary of these foreigners in their midst. Official policy towards the Hebrews changed from passive acceptance to repressive hostility and eventual enslavement. The superstitious and cruel Egyptians made life for the slaves unbearably tough:

> Then a new king, who did not know about Joseph, came to power in Egypt. 'Look,' he said to his people, 'the Israelites have become much too numerous for us. Come, we must deal shrewdly with them or they will become even more numerous and, if war breaks out, will join our enemies, fight against us and leave the country.'
>
> So they put slave masters over them to oppress them with forced labour, and they built Pithom and Rameses as store cities for Pharaoh. But the more they were oppressed, the more they multiplied and spread; so the Egyptians came to dread the Israelites and worked them ruthlessly. They made their lives bitter with hard labour in brick and mortar and with all kinds of work in the fields; in all their hard labour the Egyptians used them ruthlessly (Exodus 1:8–14).

God was aware of their misery. He set himself to find someone who could lead his cowed and defeated people to freedom, and the one he chose was quite unique: an Israelite who had been fostered by an Egyptian princess and schooled as an Egyptian aristocrat. That person's name was *Moses*, and, more than any other person, Moses was set to shape the life and consciousness of the Hebrew nation for thousands of years to come.

Moses – God's friend

The LORD said, 'I have indeed seen the misery of my people in Egypt. I have heard them crying out because of their slave drivers, and I am concerned about their suffering. So I have come down to rescue them from the hand of the Egyptians and to bring them up out of that land into a good and spacious land, a land flowing with milk and honey – the home of the Canaanites, Hittites, Amorites, Perizzites, Hivites and Jebusites. And now the cry of the Israelites has reached me, and I have seen the way the Egyptians are oppressing them. So now, go. I am sending you to Pharaoh to bring my people the Israelites out of Egypt.'

God said to Moses, 'I AM WHO I AM. This is what you are to say to the Israelites: "I AM has sent me to you" ' (Exodus 3:7–10, 14).

God revealed himself to Moses in a fresh and powerful way, calling himself 'YAHWEH' – 'The LORD'. Self-existing, needing no other creature to support him. Infinite, with inexhaustible resources and glory. Yet a personal God, willing and able to form relationships with people. Moses discovered the Lord to be at once terrifyingly powerful and tenderly loving. And he became God's friend.

This God sent Moses and his brother Aaron to challenge the might of Pharaoh's Egypt. The Pharaoh was reluctant to lose his cheap labour-force and resisted. So the Lord afflicted Egypt with ten plagues, the climax of which was the spectacular slaying of every firstborn male in the country. The only people who escaped tragedy were the Hebrew families who, on Moses' instructions, had killed a lamb and painted its blood on the doorpost of their primitive houses.

As the families cowered in their little hovels, eating the remains of the lamb, fully dressed so as to make a run for it at a moment's notice, God himself annihilated every eldest son in the land. Pharaoh temporarily relented and, at Moses' command, the children of Israel made a break for it, streaming with one mind towards the Sinai peninsula.

God had delivered his people as they had acted out another significant *prototype* or model.

They had celebrated their first passover and would repeat the event symbolically every year for thousands of years. God was showing Israel that the blood of a spotless lamb would protect them from God's judgment. This reached fulfilment when Jesus, *the* Lamb of God, would die for the sins of the world.

Pharaoh's concession to Moses was brief, within hours he mobilized his standing army to recapture the fleeing rabble of slaves. The situation was desperate, thousands of refugees squeezed against the shore of the Sea of Reeds facing the advance of professional soldiers as merciless as any mercenaries in history. Then, as night fell, the unthinkable happened.

> *Then Moses stretched out his hand over the sea, and all that night the LORD drove the sea back with a strong east wind and turned it into dry land. The waters were divided, and the Israelites went through the sea on dry ground, with a wall of water on their right and on their left (Exodus 14:21–22).*

Moses led the Israelites into the arid wasteland of the Sinai peninsula. Here in this rocky crucible God began to teach his people.

He gave them a whole series of rules and regulations found today in the books of Exodus, Leviticus, Numbers and Deuteronomy.

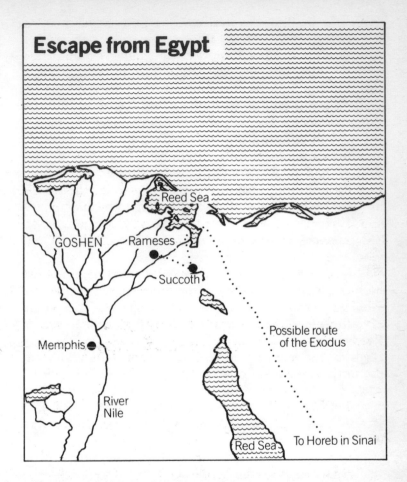

Escape from Egypt

- Reed Sea
- GOSHEN
- Rameses
- Succoth
- Possible route of the Exodus
- Memphis
- River Nile
- Red Sea
- To Horeb in Sinai

Enter the Tabernacle

Then he taught them to observe elaborate rituals which centred around a portable temple called the *tabernacle*. These rituals were pictures of the realities that would be demonstrated later in the New Testament. The details of these are intricate and complicated, but one detail is of interest here which relates back to the original 'fall' by Adam and Eve:

> *After he drove the man out, he placed on the east*
> *side of the Garden of Eden cherubim and a flaming*
> *sword flashing back and forth to guard the way to*
> *the tree of life (Genesis 3:24).*

God placed these cherubim on guard at the entrance to Eden to prevent the return of humankind to paradise.

> *Make a curtain of blue, purple and scarlet yarn and*
> *finely twisted linen, with cherubim worked into it*
> *by a skilled craftsman. . . Hang the curtain from*
> *the clasps and place the ark of the Testimony behind*
> *the curtain. The curtain will separate the Holy Place*
> *from the Most Holy Place (Exodus 26:31, 33).*

The cherubim symbolically barred the entrance to the Holy of Holies. This is a fascinating detail for reasons we will see in due course!

It's very hard for us to imagine how difficult it was for the Israelites to accept Moses' revelations. This invisible God refused to allow himself to be represented by idols carved out of wood or metal, and was difficult to understand. Whilst Moses was alone with God, the Israelites lost their nerve and made a calf out of gold to worship (read about it in Exodus 32). Yahweh had to be very patient with his juvenile people.

From Kadesh Barnea on the edge of Sinai, Moses sent spies to reconnoitre the land of Canaan. They discovered a collection of nations who were sophisticated, well armed and living in fortified cities (Numbers 13). The people were intimidated by the spies' story and petitioned Moses to let them return to Egypt rather than go on with the Lord. They had forgotten their rescue from Egypt and couldn't believe that God could rescue them from the Canaanites. So he refused to allow this faithless generation to enter the land that he had promised to them. Their wanderings in Sinai were prolonged for forty years until the next generation was grown to adulthood (Numbers 14:1–35).

Happily, two of the spies, *Joshua* and *Caleb*, refused to be unnerved by the odds against them, encouraging the people of God to keep faith and trust in his power. Under God's guidance, Israel's destiny lay in the hands of these two people.

CHAPTER 3

......

The Age of Heroes – Joshua, Judges and Samuel

MOSES died within sight of the promised land, and his successor Joshua was appointed to lead Israel into their inheritance. However, their inheritance was still densely populated with quite sophisticated and advanced people who would not simply hand it to them on a plate. What followed was a full scale invasion. After crossing the Jordan, and the miraculous destruction of Jericho, all the walled cities fell and God's people divided the land amongst themselves.

The book of Joshua describes the three main campaigns: the destruction of Ai, the march south to mop up resistance, and the sudden strike northwards to smash Hazor.

Yet Joshua is much more than a regimental history of the Israelite infantry. Two key themes dominate the book. To start with, God's people were going through a time of great change; from a nomadic to a settled lifestyle, from avoidance of conflict to engaging in vigorous warfare. Change was moving faster than people could adapt to. This book reminds us of the changeless realities that

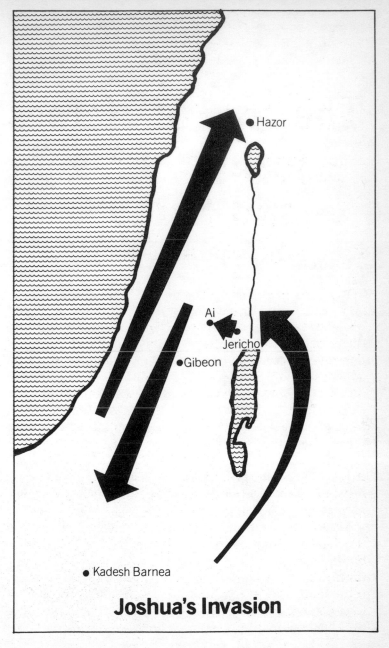

Joshua's Invasion

stabilize God's people in a changing world. There are three of them:

Firstly, God's revealed word remains true (Joshua 1:8). Secondly, God's power is still available and at work through us (Joshua 1:9) and thirdly, the Lord himself is our leader. We are on *his* side! (Joshua 5:13–15).

Our world is changing no less quickly. Change is the watchword of the modern world and it can leave us reeling with a sense of instability. Yet these three stabilizing realities are still true for God's people today. That's how we can face up to a changing world with deep peace in our hearts.

Genocide and judgment

The other key theme in Joshua is genocide! God had ordered the total annihilation of the Canaanites. In retrospect this seems cruel, but Canaanite society had degenerated to the point where God was determined that it must be destroyed. He was using the Hebrews as his weapons of judgment.

The chief source of the evil was the worship of a variety of deities known as the *Baals*. We are used to thinking of religion as a positive influence in society, but Baal worship was the opposite and an actual incitement to wickedness. Baal himself was a fairly harmless storm god, but his colleague *Molech* demanded the sacrificial death of small children when people worshipped him. The cult of *Astarte*, goddess of 'love', involved a variety of depraved sexual practices.

This is a conflict the modern Christian has in a subtly different form. Like the ancient Hebrews we find it easier to worship something we can see rather than someone we cannot! Even though we may find these alternative religions unsophisticated and even depraved, there are other things that pull at our modern hearts just as strongly. Our contemporary gods include the pursuit of wealth, possessions, prestige, sexuality and many others. We need to learn to ask the question: 'What is really controlling me?', and 'Am I still honouring the Lord in my behaviour?' Joshua teaches us not to give in to the temptation to worship what we can see at the expense of the God we can't see!

These gods eventually contributed heavily to the downfall of the Hebrew people. The Hebrews failure to annihilate the Canaanites ensured the survival of pagan religion in their promised land. In future years Yahweh would be abandoned frequently in favour of Baal worship . . . even worship of the hideous Molech became popular amongst the Israelites. The destructive pressure of idolatry would prove the eventual ruin of the Hebrews.

Judges and tribal leaders

As well as the internal pressure of idolatry, the young nation of Israel was under severe pressure from the surrounding nations. This is the key theme of the book of Judges.

> *After that whole generation had been gathered to their fathers, another generation grew up, who knew neither the* Lord *nor what he had done for Israel. Then the Israelites did evil in the eyes of the* Lord *and served the Baals. They forsook the* Lord, *the God of their fathers, who had brought them out of Egypt. They followed and worshipped various gods of the peoples around them. They provoked the* Lord *to anger because they forsook him and served Baal and the Ashtoreths. In his anger against Israel the Lord handed them over to raiders who plundered them. He sold them to their enemies all around,*

> *whom they were no longer able to resist. Whenever Israel went out to fight, the hand of the LORD was against them to defeat them, just as he had sworn to them. They were in great distress.*
>
> *Then the LORD raised up judges, who saved them out of the hands of these raiders (Judges 2:10–15, 16).*

God gave the Israelites a succession of tribal leaders called judges to help them fight off their hostile neighbours. The most significant of these were:

***Othniel*:**   Caleb's younger brother who saved Israel from the Arameans.

***Ehud*:**   A political assassin, who quietly despatched the king of Moab.

***Deborah*:**   Israel's Boadicea, who galvanized resistance to the city of Hazor.

***Gideon*:**   His specially chosen force of 300 shock troops defeated the combined forces of Midian and Amalek.

***Jephtha*:**   The 'Reckless Eric' of the Bible who held the Ammonites at bay.

***Samson*:**   The child of destiny intended to free Israel from Philistine oppression, but whose infatuation with Philistine women ensured that he never really got round to it!

All these stories are a rich source of practical instruction for us today. Whether it's the recklessness of Jephtha, or the subtle decline of Gideon, we can gain a lot from a study of these people. Perhaps Samson is the most tragic.

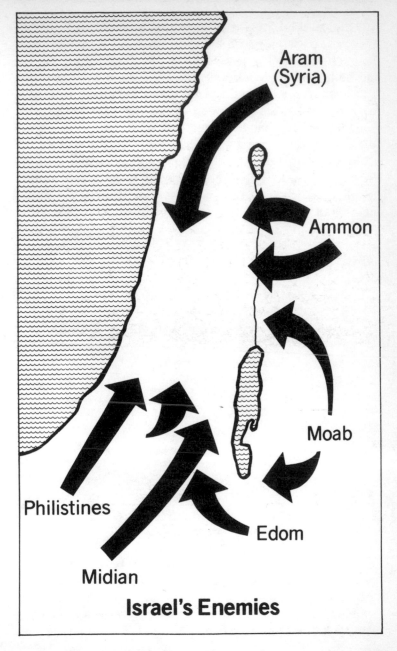

Aram (Syria)

Ammon

Moab

Philistines

Edom

Midian

Israel's Enemies

We can all think of Christians with such a lot of potential but who dissipated it because of lack of self-control. Samson was such a person.

The judges were a colourful and interesting crew! But as a system for governing God's people the *ad hoc* arrival of tribal deliverers never really inspired the nation with the confidence that they needed. The last three characters, *Abimelech*, *Jephtha* and *Samson* were great leaders but dubious characters. The books of 1 and 2 Samuel describe how the times of the judges come to a close. Samuel himself was the last of the judges but as he reached old age his obvious successors did not inspire confidence.

Samuel says 'No' to Saul

When Samuel grew old, he appointed his sons as judges for Israel. The name of his firstborn was Joel and the name of his second was Abijah, and they served at Beersheba. But his sons did not walk in his ways. They turned aside after dishonest gain and accepted bribes and perverted justice (1 Samuel 8:1).

The system of judges had failed and Israel had had enough.

So all the elders of Israel gathered together and came to Samuel at Ramah. They said to him 'You are old, and your sons do not walk in your ways; now appoint a king to lead us, such as all the other nations have' (1 Samuel 8:4–5).

It's obvious from the rest of the Old Testament that it was always God's intention to establish a king in Israel. But Israel's demand was rash and premature. They demanded, 'We want a king . . . *such as all the other nations have.'*

Their first king was *exactly* that. Gifted, attractive, tall and manly, yet unstable and in character totally unsuitable for the task. Saul failed the Lord through his own arrogance and disobedience.

Eventually Samuel confronted Saul:

> *'You acted foolishly', Samuel said. 'You have not kept the command the LORD your God gave you; if you had, he would have established your kingdom over Israel for all time. But now your kingdom will not endure; the LORD has sought out a man after his own heart and appointed him leader of his people, because you have not kept the LORD's command' (1 Samuel 13:13–14).*

The rise of David

The king that God always had in mind was a king 'after his own heart', someone who would 'role-model' God's character and rule in obedience to his will. Someone he could point to in future years and say, 'That is my kind of king!' The old judge Samuel, was led secretly to Bethlehem in Judah to find and anoint the man of God's choice. He was rather impressed by the oldest son:

> *When they arrived, Samuel saw Eliab and thought, 'Surely the LORD's annointed stands before the LORD.' But the LORD said to Samuel, 'Do not consider his appearance or his height, for I have rejected him. The LORD does not look at the things man looks at. Man looks at the outward appearance but the LORD looks at the heart' (1 Samuel 16:6–7).*

Eliab had the required physique, just like Saul, but God was looking for a person with the right heart, not the right height! The whole episode is a lesson in using the right criteria when choosing leaders for God's people.

> *So he asked Jesse, 'Are these all the sons you have?'*
> *'There is still the youngest,' Jesse answered, 'but he is tending the sheep.'*
> *Samuel said 'Send for him; we will not sit down until he arrives.'*
> *So he sent and had him brought in. He was ruddy, with a fine appearance and handsome features.*
> *Then the LORD said, 'Rise and anoint him; he is the one.'*
> *So Samuel took the horn of oil and anointed him in the presence of his brothers, and from that day on the Spirit of the LORD came upon David in power. Samuel then went to Ramah (1 Samuel 16:11–13).*

Thus David was chosen. But why was David especially someone 'after God's own heart'? He was a sinner like everyone else – what made him special? Again, why is David anointed king – many years before Saul's death? Why not just get rid of Saul? The answer to these questions will become clear as we look at the life of this remarkable person.

David came to prominence by killing a huge Philistine champion – Goliath – in single combat. Afterwards, as one of Saul's commandos he became so popular and so successful that Saul grew to hate him and tried to kill him. David lived as an outlaw for many years while still drawing Saul's victims to his hideout and offering them protection and leadership. Eventually Saul was killed in battle and David was established as king.

Building the kingdom

Here is another prototype, an Old Testament model of a reality that would emerge in the New Testament. Who else in Scripture is proclaimed ruler, whilst another ruler is still firmly in place? Who else in Scripture builds his kingdom under the nose of that ruler? Who builds not by force but by respect and love, and offers those who love him refuge and a new life? Who is known as the Son of David?

The life of David – the secretly anointed king who came into his kingdom after the death of Saul – is a model for us of the way in which Jesus is building his kingdom on earth. He is king, but the dark powers that dominate the earth are still in place. On his return he will dispose of the evil one altogether, then he will be undisputed king of all! David is the model of Jesus' style of kingdom, God's kind of king!

David was spiritually and artistically gifted as well as being an outstanding soldier. Many of the Psalms were written by him and reflect his experiences of God. Some are triumphal and joyous, others are reflective and sad. Many of David's songs focus on our pain and loneliness when we feel that God is far away. All of them are honest in a way few of us are prepared to be, the testimony of someone unafraid to be themselves in the presence of their Lord. He was a person with weaknesses that eventually almost destroyed him, but despite this he was someone that God could use and under his leadership Israel became a strong and prosperous nation. The Philistines were finally subdued and Israel could live and work in peace.

Before David died, God made him a solemn promise:

> The LORD swore an oath to David,
>   a sure oath that he will not revoke:
> 'One of your own descendants

> *I will place on your throne —*
> *if your sons keep my covenant*
>   *and the statutes I teach them,*
> *then their sons shall sit*
>   *on your throne for ever and ever.*
> *'. . . Here I will make a horn grow for*
>   *David*
>   *and set up a lamp for my anointed*
>   *one.'*
>
>   *(Psalm 132:11–12, 17)*

The promised Saviour would be one of *his* descendants.

CHAPTER 4

The Golden Age – and Decay

SAUL'S reign had been a complete disaster, yet many in Israel had good reason to be grateful to him. For example the people of Jabesh Gilead had been delivered from a humiliating defeat at the hands of Nahash the Ammonite (see 1 Samuel 11). Saul's vigorous counter attack was gratefully remembered, and the soldiers of Jabesh risked their lives to rescue Saul's body from the victorious Philistines.

On Saul's death, David's kingship was not universally acceptable. The more northern tribes distrusted the intentions of the people of Judah and declared Saul's son, Ish-Bosheth, as their king (2 Samuel 4:1 and following), but his reign soon collapsed and the whole of Israel united behind David's kingship. Yet the damage had been done and a fundamental psychologial rift had appeared in the nation. This rift was to widen as time went on.

David wisely moved his capital from Hebron to a newly captured Jebusite fortress slap in the middle of the two factions. The fortress was called Zion, he renamed it 'The City of David'. We call it Jerusalem.

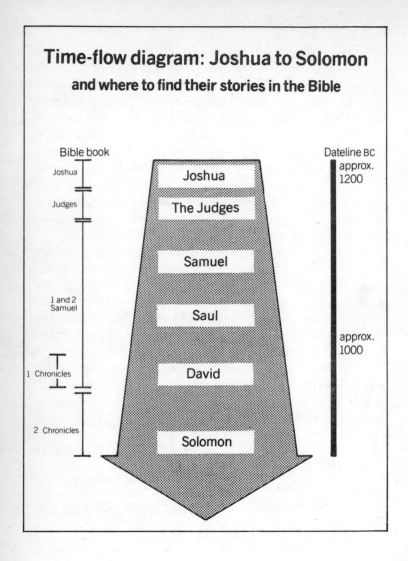

Time-flow diagram: Joshua to Solomon
and where to find their stories in the Bible

Bible book

Joshua

Judges

1 and 2 Samuel

1 Chronicles

2 Chronicles

Joshua

The Judges

Samuel

Saul

David

Solomon

Dateline BC
approx. 1200

approx. 1000

Golden days

From his base in Jerusalem, David subdued the Philistines and created a new era in Israel; for the first time in their history the Hebrews were free from the threat of invasion. His son *Solomon* inherited a stable and prosperous country with an expanding economy and cultural life. Solomon used this new era of international stability to extend his influence south to the gulf of Aquabah where he developed iron and copper mining. His net income increased to twenty-five tons of gold per annum. Not a bad salary even by today's standards! Solomon's reign was the 'golden age' in Israel's history, the full breadth of God's promises being fulfilled in them.

At this time the ancient portable 'tabernacle' faithfully preserved by the Hebrews was replaced with an impressive permanent temple with a roof made of cedarwood and walls adorned with rich treasures. Solomon also built a beautiful palace where he housed his excessive number of wives and a rather self-indulgent number of concubines!

His wisdom made him famous but his spiritual failings were disastrous for Israel. Strengthening his international treaties by marrying foreign princesses, Solomon created a cosmopolitan court where faithfulness to the Lord was hard to maintain.

> *As Solomon grew old, his wives turned his heart after other gods, and his heart was not fully devoted to the LORD his God, as the heart of David his father had been. He followed Ashtoreth the goddess of the Sidonians, and Molech the detestable god of the Ammonites (1 Kings 11:4–5).*

Like many a Christian who finds success in his or her professional life, Solomon tried to combine godliness with being an 'upwardly mobile' and urbane 'man of the world', but it was a combination that stood no chance of working. His marriages to women from outside the people of God proved an irresistibly destructive force in his life. In later years he lost his grip on spiritual reality altogether, suffering bouts of deep unhappiness. This experience strikes a chord with the book of Ecclesiastes which may have been written by Solomon.

> *I amassed silver and gold for myself, and the treasure of kings and provinces. I acquired men and women singers, and a harem as well – the delights of the heart of man. I became greater by far than anyone in Jerusalem before me. In all this my wisdom stayed with me. . .*
>
> *Yet when I surveyed all that my hands*
> *had done*
> *and what I had toiled to achieve,*
> *everything was meaningless, a chasing*
> *after the wind;*
> *nothing was gained under the sun.*
> *(Ecclesiastes 2:8–9, 11)*

Compromise sets in

Solomon's life illustrates how careful we ought to be to maintain a consistent walk with God. His early years were characterized by mature spirituality. Yet his consistency was eroded by unwise relationships. The strongest believer is only a decision away from failure. Solomon was wiser than us all and his failure is scary to say the least!

Yet, in spite of Solomon's achievements, his subjects were unhappy and did not share his enthusiasm for building, loathing the harsh labour and taxation they had to put up with. Only Judah and Benjamin remained loyal to Solomon's successor – *Rehoboam*. The rest of Israel revolted, proclaiming *Jeroboam* king.

Now the rift had widened to a gulf. God's people were two nations. Israel in the north and Judah in the south. From now on Israel and Judah have separate but inter-related histories. We will look at the national history of Israel first; it lasted exactly two hundred years!

Like Saul, Jeroboam had a fair chance to make good, in fact it was because of Solomon's failure that God actually appointed him. Here's what the book of 1 Kings says about him and a prophet of his day:

> *About that time Jeroboam was going out of Jerusa-lem, and Ahijah the prophet of Shiloh met him on the way, wearing a new cloak. The two of them were alone out in the country, and Ahijah took hold of the new cloak he was wearing and tore it into twelve pieces. Then he said to Jeroboam, 'Take ten pieces for yourself, for this is what the LORD, the God of Israel, says: "See, I am going to tear the kingdom out of Solomon's hand and give you ten tribes. But for the sake of my servant David and the city of Jerusalem, which I have chosen out of all the tribes of Israel, he will have one tribe. I will do this because they have forsaken me and worshipped Ashtoreth the goddess of the Sidonians, Chemosh the god of the Moabites, and Molech the god of the Ammonites, and have not walked in my ways, nor done what is right in my eyes, nor kept my statutes and laws as David, Solomon's father did" ' (1 Kings 11:29–33).*

Also like Saul, a silly act of disobedience started Jeroboam on the road to ruin. He had begun his reign with a big problem, because Rehoboam's capital city, Jerusalem, had a fine temple and Jeroboam's subjects had to go there to worship. Jeroboam had no capital and no temple, and the prospect of his people day-tripping to Judah worried him:

> Then Jeroboam fortified Shechem in the hill country
> of Ephraim and lived there. From there he went out
> and built up Peniel.
>
> Jeroboam thought to himself, 'The kingdom is now
> likely to revert to the house of David. If these people
> go up to offer sacrifices at the temple of the LORD
> in Jerusalem, they will again give their allegiance to
> their lord, Rehoboam king of Judah. They will kill
> me and return to King Rehoboam.'
>
> After seeking advice, the king made two golden
> calves. He said to the people, 'It is too much for you
> to go up to Jerusalem. Here are your gods, O Israel,
> who brought you up out of Egypt.' One he set up
> in Bethel and the other in Dan. And this thing
> became a sin; the people went even as far as Dan to
> worship the one there (1 Kings 12:25–30).

Jeroboam was doomed – yet he had set a precedent to be
followed by many an Israelite king; idolatry for reasons of
political convenience. Jeroboam had missed a God-given
opportunity to be as great as David. After all, God had
promised to him:

> 'However, as for you, I will take you, and you will
> rule over all that your heart desires; you will be king
> over Israel. If you do whatever I command you and
> walk in my ways and do what is right in my eyes
> by keeping my statutes and commands, as David
> my servant did, I will be with you. I will build you
> a dynasty as enduring as the one I built for David
> and will give Israel to you. I will humble David's
> descendants because of this, but not for ever'
> (1 Kings 11:37–39).

Yet Jeroboam's alternative worship sites at Bethel and
Dan were set to snare the nation of Israel for the next
two centuries.

Israel

● Samaria

● Bethel

● Jerusalem

Judah

A Divided Kingdom

Like father, like son

Jeroboam's son *Nadab* succeeded him as king. Like his father, he fell short of God's standards.

> *Nadab son of Jeroboam became king of Israel in the second year of Asa king of Judah, and he reigned over Israel for two years. He did evil in the eyes of the LORD, walking in the ways of his father and in his sin, which he had caused Israel to commit (1 Kings 15:25–26).*

This assessment of the kings of Israel is the standard one from now on, and all the kings of Israel are judged by the same standard: *Does the king serve the Baals or not, and if not, does he neglect to destroy them?*

Baasha killed Nadab and executed all of Jeroboam's remaining family. He was followed by his son *Elah*, who reigned for two years until *Zimri* killed him and wiped out *his* family. Zimri took over the throne for a whole seven days until he committed suicide rather than face death at the hands of the powerful general *Omri* who headed-up a military coup.

Things settled down a bit under King Omri who was a powerful and competent king. He lasted a whole twelve years in office! He built *Samaria* and established it as capital of Israel. He made strengthening alliances with surrounding nations and crushed the ones that wouldn't co-operate. *Moab* was one of these and was forced to pay heavy taxes to Omri:

> *Now Mesha king of Moab raised sheep, and he had to supply the king of Israel with a hundred thousand lambs and with the wool of a hundred thousand rams (2 Kings 3:4).*

A piece of archaeological evidence from Moab itself confirms this. King Mesha of Moab wrote on a stone tablet: 'Omri, king of Israel, humbled Moab for many years.'

By most standards he was a wise and successful king, but not by God's standards.

> But Omri did evil in the eyes of the LORD and sinned more than all those before him. He walked in all the ways of Jeroboam son of Nebat and in his sin, which he had caused Israel to commit, so that they provoked the LORD, the God of Israel, to anger by their worthless idols (1 Kings 16:25–26).

Omri was the worst yet, but his son *Ahab* was the worst ever! He built a temple for Baal in Samaria and institutionalized Baal worship. He also married Jezebel, a Sidonian princess and devout Baal worshipper. Once established as queen she initiated the systematic killing of the Lord's prophets.

Send in the prophet

Ever since Moses, God sent prophets to his people to keep alive his message and remind his people of the terms of the covenant they had made on Mount Horeb. These prophets crop up regularly in the Old Testament, usually acting as messengers, very rarely as miracle workers.

With the arrival of Ahab and his sinister consort Jezebel, the threat to God's people became acute. Things had gone from bad to worse and the stage was set for the arrival of a most unusual person; the first miracle-working mega-prophet since Moses:

Now Elijah, the Tishbite, from Tishbe in Gilead, said to Ahab, 'As the LORD, the God of Israel, lives, whom I serve, there will be neither dew nor rain in the next few years except at my word' (1 Kings 17:1).

What happens next, and how Elijah attempts to pull Israel back from the brink we will see in the next chapter.

CHAPTER 5

·················

To the Brink and Over It – Israel's Last Years

*E*LIJAH and Ahab had what was possibly the biggest personality clash in Old Testament history, as the first book of Kings explains:

> *So . . . Ahab went to meet Elijah. When he saw Elijah, he said to him, 'Is that you, you troubler of Israel?'*
> *'I have not made trouble for Israel,' Elijah replied. 'But you and your father's family have. You have abandoned the LORD's commands and have followed the Baals' (1 Kings 18:16–18).*

The core of the problem was the resurgence of Baal worship that Ahab and Jezebel were spearheading. Elijah's arrival was Israel's big chance to repent and get back on the rails of obedience to God's law. He was equipped for the job; with a powerful personality, an implicit trust in God and the ability to do impressive miracles. He offered Israel a simple choice:

> *So Ahab sent word throughout all Israel and*
> *assembled the prophets on Mount Carmel. Elijah*
> *went before the people and said, 'How long will you*
> *waver between two opinions? If the LORD is God,*
> *follow him; but if Baal is God, follow him' (1 Kings*
> *18:20–21).*

The climax of his life was a spectacular contest on Mount Carmel. Alone, he challenged four hundred and fifty prophets of Baal to a simple contest. Elijah won and as torrential rain fell, he ran the twenty-six miles to Jezreel in front of Ahab's chariot. In Jezreel he was threatened by Jezebel. Elijah was utterly crushed and fled to Beersheba where he promptly told the Lord that he was giving up!

Elijah – just like us

Elijah is an extremely interesting person, a very powerful prophet whose collapse shows his inner fragility: he really did think he was alone (1 Kings 18:22 and 19:10). This is a great comfort to ordinary people like you and me! As James says in the New Testament, 'Elijah was a man, just like us' (James 5:17). This is important and, although the Bible is full of heroes, they were still ordinary people, and when God calls us to out-of-the-ordinary service he promises to give us the resources we need. Elijah's collapse warns us to be wise about conserving our energy; running a marathon after spiritual combat is certainly not wise!

Then, after his collapse God took Elijah back to Horeb (1 Kings 19) where God had given the Law. For a Hebrew like this it was a journey back to his spiritual roots and a time of restoration and revival. The Christian's spiritual roots go back not to a mountain in Sinai, but to a hill outside Jerusalem. Christians find healing and renewal through what Jesus achieved on the cross. That's the place to go when we collapse and need restoring.

Elijah's experience of God working powerfully through him teaches us a significant lesson about the role of 'miracle-working mega-prophets': At three key moments in history such a ministry has arisen. Firstly the time of Moses, then in the work of Elisha and Elijah, and finally in the lives of Jesus and his apostles. In between these times miracles do happen, but not routinely. God seems to concentrate intense miracle-working into the lives of very strategic individuals at crucial moments in history. Perhaps we are barking up the wrong tree if we expect everyday life to be a miracle-a-minute experience!

As things stood, the problems in Israel went so deep that the powerful work of Elijah and his apprentice Elisha only just held back the tide. Ahab's dynasty was destroyed in another coup led by *Jehu*. Zealous for the Lord he never lived up to expectations and failed to eliminate the Baals from Israel. After Jehu the dam broke, and a new tide of wickedness came pouring in. The northern kingdom was lining up for destruction!

The rise of the Assyrians

Up until now Israel's greatest external enemy had been the Arameans (Syrians) in the north. During this period all this changed quite drastically. In 852 BC a loose coalition of eleven nations including Aram were smashed by the mighty *Assyrians* . . . a vigorous superpower with a deliberate policy of expanding their empire.

They were led by implacable warrior kings who were warlike, vicious and proud of their expertise in torture. From now on Assyria was the big enemy. During Jehu's reign the Assyrians clamped down on Israel and extracted heavy 'protection money' (or tributes).

The Bible tells us that God does not move in judgment without declaring his intentions through the prophets

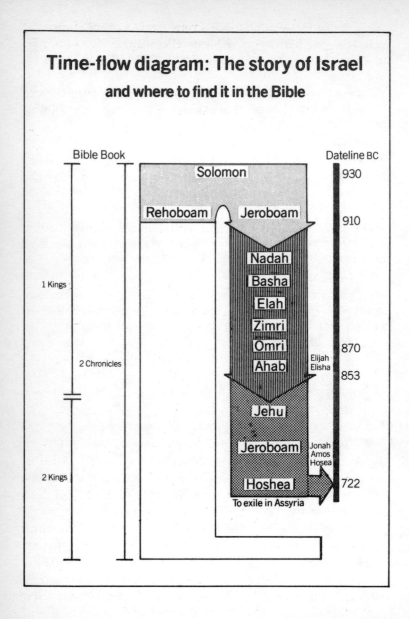

Time-flow diagram: The story of Israel
and where to find it in the Bible

Bible Book

Dateline BC

Solomon

930

Rehoboam   Jeroboam

910

1 Kings

Nadah

Basha

Elah

Zimri

Omri

870

Ahab   Elijah
              Elisha   853

2 Chronicles

Jehu

Jeroboam   Jonah
                  Amos
                  Hosea

2 Kings

Hoshea   722

To exile in Assyria

first: 'Surely the Sovereign LORD does nothing without revealing his plan to his servants, the prophets' (Amos 3:7).

Three key people addressed the problems of Israel:

Jonah: An adviser to Jeroboam II, who spent some time in the Assyrian capital city doing missionary work.

Amos: A native of Judah, who worked as a missionary in Israel drawing attention to the nations' sinful social inequalities.

Hosea: Was concerned with Israel's turning away and increasing 'apostasy', and prophesied against it.

As Assyrian power increased, the prophets' warnings about Israel's destruction grew more urgent. King *Menahem* was terrorized by Assyria:

> *Then Pul king of Assyria invaded the land, and Menahem gave him a thousand talents of silver to gain his support and strengthen his own hold on the kingdom (2 Kings 15:19).*

This severe ransom served two purposes: it lined the coffers of King Pul (whose other name was Tiglath-Pileser III) and rendered Israel incapable of hiring a mercenary army to defend it. Thus neutered, Israel was helpless to defend itself! But there was worse to come: as Assyria grew in experience the system of extracting crippling taxes like this gave way to a more vicious but efficient way of maintaining order in the empire. Conquered peoples were deported in huge numbers and settled in strange countries to serve as slaves. Cut off from their nationalistic roots the captives became demoralized and lost the will and organization to fight back.

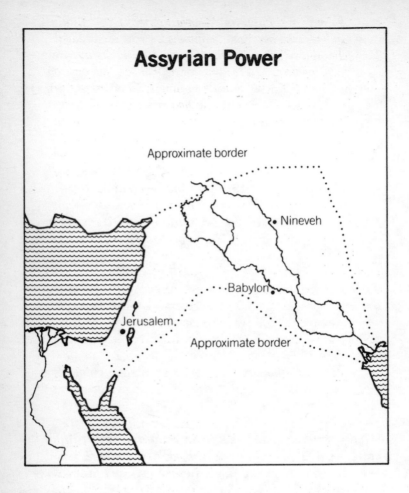

The axe falls on Israel

During the reign of *Hoshea* the axe fell, the prophet's warnings were fulfilled, and the people of Israel went into exile.

Shalmaneser king of Assyria came up to attack Hoshea, who had been Shalmaneser's vassal and had paid him tribute. But the king of Assyria discovered that Hoshea was a traitor, for he had sent envoys to So king of Egypt, and he no longer paid tribute to the king of Assyria, as he had done year by year. Therefore Shalmaneser seized him and put him in prison. The king of Assyria invaded the entire land, marched against Samaria and laid siege to it for three years. In the ninth year of Hoshea, the king of Assyria captured Samaria and deported the Israelites to Assyria. He settled them in Halah, in Gozan on the Habor River and in the towns of the Medes (2 Kings 17:3–6).

The northern kingdom of Israel had ceased to exist and the deported people were absorbed into the Assyrian empire. They *never* reappeared in human history except in a few mystical myths – just about every nation with delusions of grandeur traces its ancestry back to the 'lost tribes of Israel'.

The lost tribes remained lost and Scripture gives us a reason:

All this took place because the Israelites had sinned against the LORD their God, who had brought them out of Egypt from under the power of Pharaoh king of Egypt. They worshipped other gods and followed the practices of the nations the LORD had driven out before them, as well as the practices that the kings of Israel had introduced. The Israelites secretly did things against the LORD their God that were not right. From watchtower to fortified city they built themselves high places in all their towns. They set up sacred stones and Asherah poles on every high hill and under every spreading tree. At every high place they burned incense, as the nations whom the

*LORD had driven out before them had done. They
did wicked things that provoked the LORD to anger.
They worshipped idols, though the LORD had said,
'You shall not do this.' The LORD warned Israel and
Judah through all his prophets and seers: 'Turn from
your evil ways. Observe my commands and decrees,
in accordance with the entire Law that I commanded
your fathers to obey and that I delivered to you
through my servants the prophets.'*

*But they would not listen and were as stiff-necked
as their fathers, who did not trust in the LORD their
God. They rejected his decrees and the covenant he
had made with their fathers and the warnings he
had given them. They followed worthless idols and
themselves became worthless. They imitated the
nations around them although the LORD had ordered
them, 'Do not do as they do', and they did the things
the LORD had forbidden them to do. They forsook
all the commands of the LORD their God and made
for themselves two idols cast in the shape of calves
and an Asherah pole. They bowed down to all the
starry hosts, and they worshipped Baal. They sacrificed their sons and daughters in the fire. They
practised divination and sorcery and sold themselves
to do evil in the eyes of the LORD, provoking him
to anger'* (2 Kings 17:7–17).

Though Israel's fall is attributed to idolatry, their failure
to do good is also blamed. Amos made this clear in his
scorching indictment of the nation (Amos 2:6–16). Israel
shows us that what you believe with your heart deter-
mines how you behave with your life. When people
believe the wrong things, their behaviour goes wrong
too.

So much for Israel, but what about our nation? If God
is shunted off to the periphery of people's thinking, and
any old set of ideas is put in his place, how long will it

be before our behaviour deteriorates to the point when we qualify for the same treatment as Israel?

So much for us, but what about King Rehoboam of Judah whom we left in chapter 4? Did he do any better than Jeroboam?

CHAPTER 6

······················

Judah – Over the Brink and Back Again

*F*ROM the fall of Samaria to the brutal Assyrians in 722 BC we now go back in time almost exactly two hundred years to the division of the kingdom of Israel and Judah during the mid 900s BC.

We've seen the fate of Jeroboam's and successive dynasties in Israel. How did Solomon's son Rehoboam get on?

Well, he had already started badly. Having threatened the population with higher taxation and more forced labour than had been known under Solomon, he then lost ten-twelfths of his workforce immediately when Israel declared independence! In his stupidity Rehoboam squandered the fruits of Solomon's wisdom in twenty-four hours flat.

> *The king answered the people harshly. Rejecting the advice given him by the elders, he followed the advice of young men and said, 'My father made your yoke heavy; I will make it even heavier. My father scourged you with whips; I will scourge you with*

scorpions.' So the king did not listen to the people, for this turn of events was from the LORD, *to fulfil the word the* LORD *had spoken to Jeroboam son of Nebat through Ahijah the Shilonite.*

When all Israel saw that the king refused to listen to them, they answered the king:

> *'What share do we have in David,*
> *what part in Jesse's son?*
> *To your tents, O Israel!*
> *Look after your own house, O David!'*
>
> (1 Kings 12:13–17)

The good and the great

Soon the Egyptians, under Pharaoh Sheshonk I (Shishak), carried off Solomon's entire wealth! Again, it is the first book of Kings that recounts the events:

> *In the fifth year of King Rehoboam, Shishak king of Egypt attacked Jerusalem. He carried off the treasures of the temple of the* LORD *and the treasures of the royal palace. He took everything, including all the gold shields Solomon had made (1 Kings 14:25–26).*

That little phrase 'he took everything' sums up Rehoboam's contribution to the work of God, and it tells us some important things about being 'great'. Greatness, even if it is created by God, is no guarantee of continued greatness. It is easy for fools to squander the richness of previous generations. If *we* are not careful with our spiritual inheritance, it will evaporate. We need to humbly seek God, obey him, and remain open to his leading and his ways.

Despite the efforts of fools like Rehoboam, the Lord

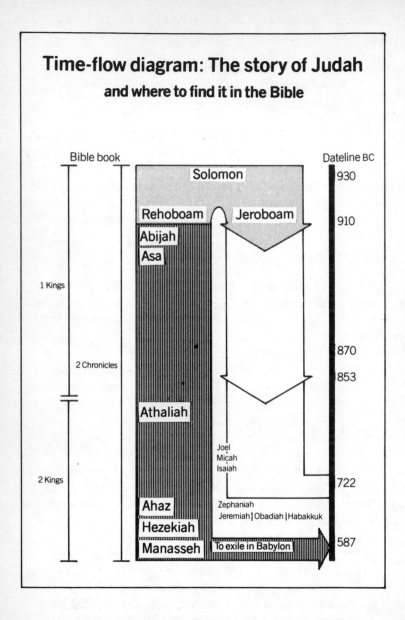

Time-flow diagram: The story of Judah
and where to find it in the Bible

Bible book

Dateline BC

Solomon — 930

Rehoboam | Jeroboam — 910

Abijah

Asa

1 Kings

2 Chronicles

870

853

Athaliah

Joel
Micah
Isaiah

2 Kings

722

Ahaz

Zephaniah
Jeremiah | Obadiah | Habakkuk

Hezekiah

Manasseh | To exile in Babylon — 587

does not forsake David's descendants. As Judah's history unfolds, the Lord keeps one promise very faithfully.

> *Your house and your kingdom shall endure for ever before me, your throne shall be established for ever (2 Samuel 7:16).*

While the people of Israel saw five distinct families have a go at the monarchy in turn, Judah always had a direct descendant of King David on the throne. As time went on, even though some of David's descendants were villains in the extreme, God kept his promise to make the Davidic dynasty the most significant monarchy in the world.

High places

Abijah succeeded Rehoboam as king and followed in his footsteps.

> *He committed all the sins his father had done before him; his heart was not fully devoted to the LORD his God, as the heart of David his forefather had been (1 Kings 15:3).*

He was a failure, because he did not live up to the standards set by David. From this point onwards, this became the test of success or failure in a Judean king – did he walk in the footsteps of David? Here, for example, is the verdict on King Asa:

> *Asa did what was right in the eyes of the LORD, as his father David had done. He expelled the male shrine-prostitutes from the land and got rid of all the idols his fathers had made. He even deposed his grandmother Maacah from her position as queen*

mother, because she had made a repulsive Asherah pole. Asa cut the pole down and burned it in the Kidron Valley. Although he did not remove the high places, Asa's heart was fully committed to the LORD all his life' (1 Kings 15:11–14).

King Asa was a 'David-like' king, but failed in one vital respect. He did not remove the 'high places'. These were small temples and rallying points for pagan worship. God hated them, but only one king ever had the courage to completely remove them.

There are 'high places' in our own lives. It takes real courage and willpower to attack them and the failure of many Judaean kings mirrors our failure to strip out the last strongholds of the old paganism within us all. Yet the challenge of the New Testament is to do just that. (See Ephesians 4:20–24.)

Although David's dynasty remained intact it was not without its villains. *Athaliah* is the 'Lady Macbeth' of 2 Kings (see 2 Kings 11) annihilating her own family in order to inherit the throne. She discovered that one little boy had survived, but was unable to prevent him being crowned in a military coup backed by the priesthood.

King *Ahaz* was the first king of Judah to sacrifice his son to the god Molech. The fruit of Baal worship in Judah began to emerge.

Ahaz was twenty years old when he became king, and he reigned in Jerusalem for sixteen years. Unlike David his father, he did not do what was right in the eyes of the LORD his God. He walked in the ways of the kings of Israel and even sacrificed his son in the fire, following the detestable ways of the nations the LORD had driven out before the Israel-ites. He offered sacrifices and burned incense at the high places, on the hilltops and under every spread-ing tree (2 Kings 16:2–4).

Ahaz had to live with the threat of rising Assyrian power. Repeated attacks on the strategic Syrian capital, Damascus, sent him scuttling up north to talk to Tiglath-Pileser III and ask him nicely not to crush his kingdom. The Assyrian backed off but only after forcing Judah to be subject to its gods. Ahaz returned with a drawing of an Assyrian altar to be erected in the temple of Jerusalem.

Hezekiah and Isaiah

Somehow, Ahaz's son *Hezekiah* managed to break out of the mould of Jewish kings. He was godly and courageous.

> In the third year of Hoshea son of Elah king of Israel, Hezekiah son of Ahaz king of Judah began to reign. He was twenty-five years old when he became king and he reigned in Jerusalem twenty-nine years. His mother's name was Abijah daughter of Zechariah. He did what was right in the eyes of the LORD just as his father David had done. He removed the high places, smashed the sacred stones and cut down the Asherah poles. He broke into pieces the bronze snake Moses had made, for up to that time the Israelites had been burning incense to it. (It was called Nehushtan.)
>
> Hezekiah trusted in the LORD the God of Israel. There was no-one like him among all the kings of Judah, either before him or after him. He held fast to the LORD and did not cease to follow him; he kept the commands the LORD had given Moses. And the LORD was with him; he was successful in whatever he undertook. He rebelled against the king of Assyria and did not serve him. From watchtower to fortified city, he defeated the Philistines, as far as Gaza and its territory (2 Kings 18:1–8).

This was too much for Assyria; fresh from demolishing Samaria and deporting the entire population of Israel, the Assyrians moved in on Judah. A massive army led by Sennacherib advanced on the major cities and destroyed Judah's second city of Lachish . . . then he moved on to Jerusalem. Even though Hezekiah was ready for Sennacherib, having made extensive preparations to resist invasion, it still needed a miracle to deliver Jerusalem:

> That night the angel of the LORD went out and put to death a hundred and eighty-five thousand men in the Assyrian camp. When the people got up the next morning – there were all the dead bodies! So Sennacherib king of Assyria broke camp and withdrew. He returned to Nineveh and stayed there (2 Kings 19:35–36).

The prophet *Isaiah* was in his heyday during Hezekiah's reign. His book records his messages from God. Many of these concern the coming Messiah, like the one we often hear at Christmas.

> Therefore the LORD himself will give you a sign: The virgin will be with child and will give birth to a son, and will call him Immanuel (Isaiah 7:14).

The rot sets in again

Hezekiah and Isaiah represent the pinnacle of Jewish history after David. From then on it was downhill all the way. Hezekiah's son *Manasseh* took Judah back to square one and beyond!

> He rebuilt the high places his father Hezekiah had destroyed; he also erected altars to Baal and made an Asherah pole, as Ahab king of Israel had done.

He bowed down to all the starry hosts and worship-
ped them. He built altars in the temple of the LORD,
of which the LORD had said, 'In Jerusalem I will
put my Name.' In both courts of the temple of the
LORD he built altars to all the starry hosts. He
sacrificed his own son in the fire, practised sorcery
and divination, and consulted mediums and spirit-
ists. He did much evil in the eyes of the LORD,
provoking him to anger.

He took the carved Asherah pole he had made and
put it in the temple, of which the LORD had said to
David and to his son Solomon, 'In this temple and
in Jerusalem, which I have chosen out of all the
tribes of Israel, I will put my Name for ever. I will
not again make the feet of the Israelites wander from
the land I commanded them and will keep the whole
Law that my servant Moses gave them.' But the
people did not listen. Manasseh led them astray, so
that they did more evil than the nations the LORD
had destroyed before the Israelites (2 Kings 21:3–9).

The theme is familiar, the fragility of godliness and blessing, and the speed of its decline when God is pushed to
the edges of national life. This fragility is a key theme in
the whole Old Testament:

Part of God's purpose for Israel was to demonstrate
the completeness of the fall of man, that he would
continue to fall even in the most favourable circum-
stances.[1]

The Old Testament constantly underlines how wicked
men and women have become – while the New Testament constantly proclaims that God's grace can forgive
and restore sinful people.

Assyria's last great king was *Ashurbanipal*, and after his
death Nineveh fell to a combined force of Babylonians

and Medes, who breached the city's defences by using floodwaters from the .Tigris. The prophecy of Nahum had been fulfilled. Babylon now became the dominant superpower in the ancient world.

Meanwhile the Judaean people were in constant moral decline. A whole series of prophets brought God's word to a backsliding and deeply apostate nation.

Isaiah: Speaks of the present destruction, and future beauty of Jerusalem.

Joel: Foresees destruction, and the coming of the Spirit to God's people.

Obadiah: Tells how God will punish the Edomites.

Micah: Saw a future full of doom, but a ruler emerging from Bethlehem.

Habakkuk: Couldn't believe God would use Babylon to punish Judah, yet finds deep faith and peace in the face of the unthinkable!

Zephaniah: Pronounces God's judgment on the nations, but proclaims the restoration of Jerusalem.

Malachi: Calls people to holiness, while promising that God will move in judgment as well as restoration.

On the whole it is the writer of the books of Kings who sums up their collective lesson:

> *Therefore this is what the LORD, the God of Israel says: I am going to bring such disasters on Jerusalem and Judah that the ears of everyone who hears of it will tingle. I will stretch out over Jerusalem the*

*measuring line used against Samaria and the plumb-
line used against the house of Ahab. I will wipe out
Jerusalem as one wipes out a dish, wiping it and
turning it upside-down (2 Kings 21:12–13).*

By the rivers of Babylon

The prophet Jeremiah continued to warn Judah of its
inevitable destruction. He had a tough job and nobody
believed him. But God consoled him with a new vision
of the future – a time when God would start again with
humankind.

> *'The time is coming,' declares the* Lord,
> > *'when I will make a new covenant with the house
> > of Israel*
> > *and with the house of Judah. . .*
> *'This is the covenant that I will make
> > with the house of Israel*
> *after that time,' declares the* Lord.
> *'I will put my law in their minds
> and write it on their hearts.*
> *I will be their God,
> > and they will be my people.*
> *No longer will a man teach his neighbour,
> > or a man his brother, saying, "Know the* Lord,*"
> because they will all know me,
> > from the least of them to the greatest,'*
> > > > *declares the* Lord.
> *'For I will forgive their wickedness
> and will remember their sins no more.'*
> > > > *(Jeremiah 31:31, 33–34)*

In three successive devastating campaigns the new
superpower Babylon, under King *Nebuchadnezzar*, sent
virtually the whole population of Judah into exile. In the

last campaign Nebuchadnezzar destroyed Jersualem and razed the temple to the ground.

Jeremiah, left behind with the poorer people, poured out his misery in the book of Lamentations. For those on the forced marches to Babylon the exile was a traumatic experience.

> *By the rivers of Babylon we sat and wept*
> *   when we remembered Zion.*
> *There on the poplars*
> *   we hung our harps,*
> *for there our captors asked us for songs,*
> *   our tormentors demanded songs of joy;*
> *   they said, 'Sing us one of the songs of Zion!'*
> *How can we sing the songs of the* LORD
> *   while in a foreign land?*
>
> (Psalm 137:1–4)

But despite the tragedy, not everything was hopeless. God had intended the prophecies of men like Micah to ring in their ears. He said:

> *Marshal your troops, O city of troops,*
> *   for a siege is laid against us.*
> *They will strike Israel's ruler*
> *   on the cheek with a rod.*
>
> *'But you, Bethlehem, Ephrathah,*
> *   though you are small among the clans of Judah,*
> *out of you will come for me*
> *   one who will be ruler over Israel,*
> *whose origins are from of old,*
> *   from ancient times.'*
>
> *Therefore Israel will be abandoned*
> *   until the time when she who is in*
> *   labour gives birth*

and the rest of his brothers return
  to join the Israelites.

He will stand and shepherd his flock
  in the strength of the LORD,
  in the majesty of the name of the
    LORD *his God.*
And they will live securely, for then his
    greatness
  will reach to the ends of the earth.
  And he will be their peace.

(Micah 5:1–5)

So the promised deliverer would be born of a virgin (Isaiah 7:14), and in Bethlehem!

Notes

1. H. L. Ellison, *The Message of the Old Testament* (Paternoster Press, 1969).

CHAPTER 7

....

To Babylon and Back

━━━━━━━━━

A small residue of people remained in Judah after Nebuchadnezzar's last raid. As we have seen, Jeremiah himself was left behind, still ministering to his people. He remarks:

> *How deserted lies the city,*
> *once so full of people!*
> *How like a widow is she,*
> *who once was great among the*
> *nations!*
> *She who was once queen among the*
> *provinces*
> *has now become a slave.*
>
> *(Lamentations 1:1)*

In Babylon many of the exiles found themselves doing forced labour on the banks of the Euphrates. The prophet *Ezekiel* was one of these. The Lord comforted the Jews through him by revealing a mystical blueprint for a future Jewish state.

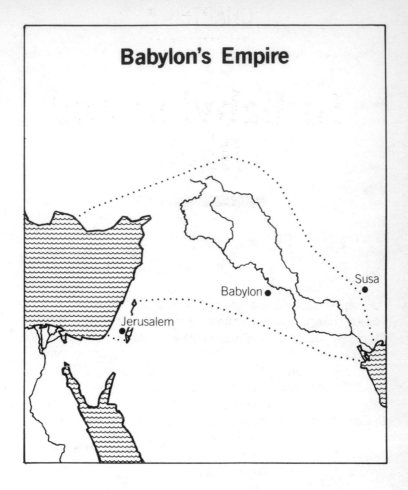

Babylon's Empire

Susa

Babylon ●

Jerusalem ●

When the state of Israel went into exile it was lost for ever. When Judah went into exile the people retained their hope for the future – even in dire circumstances. This was the work of Jeremiah and Ezekiel. In Jerusalem and Babylon respectively they testified to the fact that God had not deserted Judah.

The time-bomb stops ticking

Israel disappeared without trace because it lost the prophetic voice, and with it its distinct identity as the people of God. God stopped speaking and his people fell apart. Judah survived because God kept it supplied with men who spoke his word. In the clichéd movie image, you always know when a time-bomb will explode because it stops ticking! You can draw similar conclusions when God stops speaking.

Elijah and Elisha had been given a spectacular miraculous ministry in order to stop the slide into unbelief and apostasy. They only partly succeeded, and the destruction of Israel followed soon after them. Fascinatingly, in view of the current interest in 'signs and wonders' ministry today, God only supplied Judah with his prophetic word, unattested by the miraculous. The Jews survived the captivity and eventually returned to Judah. If the spectacular displays of an Elijah failed in his day, would it succeed in ours? A comparison of the effect of Elijah on Israel, with the impact of Jeremiah and Ezekiel on the Jews in Babylon would suggest that God's word is pretty powerful on its own!

Notwithstanding, God revealed himself to the young Ezekiel in very dramatic ways:

> In the thirtieth year, in the fourth month on the fifth day, while I was among the exiles by the Kebar River, the heavens were opened and I saw visions of God. . .
>
> Above the expanse over their heads was what looked like a throne of sapphire, and high above on the throne was a figure like that of a man. I saw that from what appeared to be his waist up he looked like glowing metal, as if full of fire, and that from there down he looked like fire; and brilliant light surrounded him (Ezekiel 1:1, 26–27).

Meanwhile God was helping Jeremiah to understand precisely what he was going to do:

> This is what the LORD says: 'When seventy years are completed for Babylon, I will come to you and fulfil my gracious promise to bring you back to this place. For I know the plans I have for you,' declares the LORD, 'plans to prosper you and not to harm you, plans to give you hope and a future. Then you will call upon me and come and pray to me, and I will listen to you. You will seek me and find me when you seek me with all your heart' (Jeremiah 29:10–13).

Daniel's remarkable experiences

Whilst many exiles were subjected to forced labour, it wasn't all bad. Some were fortunate and got plum jobs in the court of Nebuchadnezzar. *Daniel* was one of these and in due course he rose to the dizzy heights of the upper civil service in Babylon. Meanwhile Belshazzar had become king and God gave a special message to him through Daniel.

> King Belshazzar gave a great banquet for a thousand of his nobles and drank wine with them. While Belshazzar was drinking his wine, he gave orders to bring in the gold and silver goblets that Nebuchadnezzar his father had taken from the temple in Jerusalem, so that the king and his nobles, his wives and his concubines might drink from them. So they brought in the gold goblets that had been taken from the temple of God in Jerusalem, and the king and his nobles, his wives and his concubines drank from them. As they drank the wine, they praised the gods of gold and silver, of bronze,

iron, wood and stone.

Suddenly the fingers of a human hand appeared and wrote on the plaster of the wall, near the lampstand in the royal palace. The king watched the hand as it wrote. His face turned pale and he was so frightened that his knees knocked together and his legs gave way. . .

This is the inscription that was written:

MENE, MENE, TEKEL, PARSIN

(Daniel 5:1–6, 25).

Daniel was able to unravel this curious vision, it was the death sentence Babylon had been long awaiting! Belshazzar had gone too far.

This is what these words mean:

Mene: *God has numbered the days of your reign and brought it to an end.*

Tekel: *You have been weighed on the scales and found wanting.*

Peres: *Your kingdom is divided and given to the Medes and Persians.*

(Daniel 5:26–28)

To the east of Babylon, *Cyrus* king of Persia was constructing an empire of his own. His army marched on Babylon and its defences were outwitted very quickly; the crafty Persians diverted the Euphrates river which flowed right through the city and marched up the dried river bed. Babylon was outwitted, and demolished. It has never been inhabited since and today is just a heap of rubble, just as Jeremiah predicted.

> *So desert creatures and hyenas will*
>   *live there,*
>   *and there the owl will dwell.*
> *It will never again be inhabited*
>   *or lived in from generation to generation.*
>
> *(Jeremiah 50:39)*

The return to Jerusalem

Cyrus ruled from the borders of Greece to the borders of India. He also passed laws allowing religious freedom in his empire. In particular he authorized the Jews' return to Jerusalem.

> *In the first year of Cyrus king of Persia, in order to fulfil the word of the LORD spoken by Jeremiah, the LORD moved the heart of Cyrus king of Persia to make a proclamation throughout his realm and to put it in writing:*
>   *'This is what Cyrus king of Persia says:*
>   *' "The LORD, the God of heaven, has given me all the kingdoms of the earth and he has appointed me to build a temple for him at Jerusalem in Judah. Anyone of his people among you – may his God be with him, and let him go up to Jerusalem in Judah and build the temple of the LORD, the God of Israel, the God who is in Jerusalem" ' (Ezra 1:1–3).*

About forty thousand people responded and, led by *Zerubbabel*, they marched back home to rebuild the temple. However opposition from local people stopped the work until a new king, *Darius*, urged its recommencement. Unknown to the king an invisible power was at work in his formulation of foreign policy. Much earlier than this Daniel had discovered a promise from scripture about the exile and started praying.

> *I, Daniel, understood from the Scriptures, according to the word of the LORD given to Jeremiah the prophet, that the desolation of Jerusalem would last seventy years. So I turned to the LORD God and pleaded with him, in prayer and petition, in fasting, and in sackcloth and ashes.*
>
> *I prayed to the LORD my God and confessed . . .* (Daniel 9:2–4).

The prayer recounted in Daniel 9:4–19 is one of the most effective prayers in the Bible. Daniel could pray with strong faith because he knew that what he was asking was the revealed will of God. We can pray like him too, it means learning to pray with our Bibles open and asking the Lord to honour the promises that we find there. The Bible is full of the kind of prayer that seems to be reminding God of his promises! Why not try it?

Daniel's prayers were heard, the local resistance was crushed with a new directive from the king, and God's people were roused to new effort by the ministry of two new prophets in Jerusalem:

Haggai: Urged the people to get back to building the temple.

Zechariah: Held out a vision of the future spiritual renewal of God's people.

Meanwhile in the gorgeous city of Susa, the Persian capital, Darius was succeeded by *Xerxes*. After being humiliated by his wife, Vashti, Xerxes decided to replace her. So he organized a beauty contest. The winner was a beautiful Jewess called *Esther*.

This mysterious woman became God's agent in preventing a catastrophe. Unknown to anyone, Xerxes' chief official, Haman, was hatching a plot to destroy the Jews. Esther used her looks, and her cunning, to discredit and head off the holocaust. She succeeded, and God's people survived.

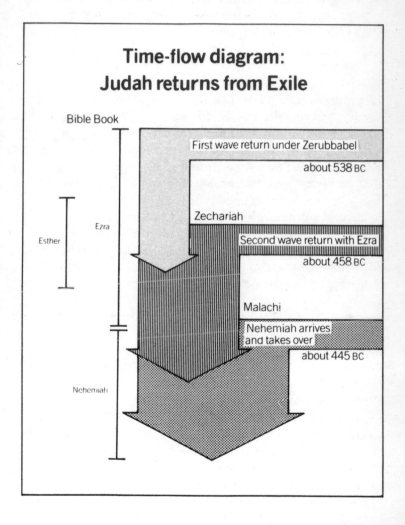

Time-flow diagram:
Judah returns from Exile

Bible Book

First wave return under Zerubbabel

about 538 BC

Zechariah

Second wave return with Ezra

about 458 BC

Malachi

Nehemiah arrives and takes over

about 445 BC

Ezra

Esther

Nehemiah

Re-building Jerusalem

Xerxes' successor *Artaxerxes* saw the second wave of Jews return to Jerusalem under Ezra . . . Artaxerxes offered him an armed guard for the dangerous journey but Ezra refused. He explained why later:

> *Ezra arrived in Jerusalem in the fifth month of the seventh year of the king. He had begun his journey from Babylon on the first day of the first month and he arrived in Jerusalem on the first day of the fifth month, for the good hand of his God was upon him. For Ezra had devoted himself to the study and observance of the Law of the LORD, and to teaching its decrees and laws in Israel (Ezra 7:8–10).*

Artaxerxes' butler was a Jew named *Nehemiah*. The king sent him to galvanize the work of rebuilding the walls of Jerusalem. He completed the work in fifty-two days, against fierce opposition.

> *When our enemies heard that we were aware of their plot and that God had frustrated it, we all returned to the wall, each to his own work.*
> *From that day on, half of my men did the work while the other half were equipped with spears, shields, bows and armour. The officers posted themselves behind all the people of Judah who were building the wall. Those who carried materials did their work with one hand and held a weapon in the other, and each of the builders wore his sword at his side as he worked. But the man who sounded the trumpet stayed with me (Nehemiah 4:15–18).*

Eventually Jerusalem was rebuilt and the land of Judah recolonized, yet the prophets' dramatic predictions of the recovery of their former glory were clearly not fulfilled.

This reborn nation was pathetically small and powerless – a mere province in a much greater empire. At this time the prophet *Malachi* wrote the final book in the Old Testament. In it the gaze of God's people is directed forwards, beyond the near future, to the coming of the promised deliverer:

> *'See, I will send my messenger, who will prepare the way before me. Then suddenly the* Lord *you are seeking will come to his temple; the messenger of the covenant, whom you desire, will come,' says the Lord Almighty (Malachi 3:1).*

The last of the prophets

After Malachi the prophets cease transmissions. The Persian empire was swallowed whole by that of Alexander the Great. On his death the power vacuum was eventually filled by the aggressive and energetic Romans. The Greek language had become the common language throughout the world, rather like English is today. Roman efficiency created a road system that made international communications possible on a previously undreamed of scale.

At this time the word of God, silent for so long, burst into the life of a rather unusual man from the hill country of Judah. His name was *John the Baptist*. This last of the old-style prophets was the one destined to prepare the way for the Lord as Malachi had promised. The flow of Old Testament story leads directly to Jesus:

> *In the past God spoke to our forefathers through the prophets at many times and in various ways, but in these last days he has spoken to us by his Son, whom he appointed heir of all things, and through whom he made the universe. The Son is the radiance of*

> God's glory and the exact representation of his
> being, sustaining all things by his powerful word.
> After he had provided purification for sins, he sat
> down at the right hand of the Majesty in heaven
> (Hebrews 1:1–3).

That is, Jesus, the Son of God, whose central work was
to die on the cross for us.

Do you remember the Fall? Adam and Eve exiled and
forbidden to return by the awesome cherubim. Do you
remember those same creatures being woven into the
curtain of the tabernacle by Moses – symbols of the path-
way into God's presence being blocked? Let's remind
ourselves of what happened on the cross:

> With a loud cry, Jesus breathed his last. The curtain
> of the temple was torn in two from top to bottom.
> And when the centurion, who stood there in front
> of Jesus, heard his cry and saw how he died, he
> said, 'Surely this man was the Son of God!' (Mark
> 15:37–39).

The curtain has gone, by his one sacrifice on the cross
Jesus the Christ has demolished the barrier between God
and humankind.

Hallelujah!

CHAPTER 8

A Sabbath Day's Walk

*J*ESUS and Paul knew their Old Testaments backwards, and I hope this sketch will stimulate you to begin catching up with the first three-quarters of your Bible! You will find that like those people who walked to Emmaus with Jesus the process will deepen your knowledge of Christ himself.

You can begin the process now by following the reading guide given at the back of the book. This will take you through the Old Testament story in three months. It is not a guide to the whole Old Testament, but to the basic storyline that runs through it.

Then you could take the plunge and take up the challenge of studying one of the Old Testament books in detail. Why not start with Genesis? But don't get bogged down with trying to read each book in the Old Testament in turn. Most people give up somewhere in Leviticus.

Finally, though a lot of the Bible is straightforward to understand, some parts present problems. Don't give up or stop probing and asking questions. Next to the Holy Spirit your greatest ally is your curiosity! Remember: 'It is the glory of God to conceal a matter, but to search out a matter is the glory of kings' (Proverbs 25:2).

In the first study we introduced the two concepts of 'prototypes' and 'promises'. Here is a summary of those two as covered in this booklet.

Prototypes (sometimes called 'types')

These are patterns set into the story itself that in some way model for us the way God has chosen to deal with people through Christ. However, you have to be careful in spotting them in the text, some Christians are so crazy and excited about the idea that they see everything as a 'type of Christ'. A good way to avoid mistakes here is to look at what the *New* Testament says about an *Old* Testament story. If the New Testament explains something in the Old as being a model of the way God works *then* you are dealing with a prototype.

We have focused on four prototypes in these studies:

a. The flood: A model of world judgment. (See Matthew 24:36–39 and 2 Peter 2:4–9.)

b. Abraham: A model of the life of faith. (See Hebrews 11:8–12.)

c. Passover: A model of salvation by the blood of a lamb. (See 1 Corinthians 5:7.)

d. David: A model of God's kind of king. (See Mark 12:35–37 and Acts 13:22.)

There are many others, have fun finding them!

Promises

The Old Testament is full of specific promises and predictions about the life of Jesus the Saviour of the world. We have only looked at a few of these, focusing on the fact that they get more specific as the story unfolds.

THE SON OF A WOMAN	Genesis 3:14–15
THE SON OF ABRAHAM	Genesis 12:1–4
THE SON OF DAVID	Psalm 132
THE SON OF A VIRGIN	Isaiah 7:14
BORN IN BETHLEHEM	Micah 5:2
THE SON OF MAN	Daniel 7:13
THE SON OF GOD	Hebrews 1:1–4

Reading guide through the Old Testament

*I*F only we could travel through time like Doctor Who, think of the fascinating things we would see: King John reluctantly signing the Magna Carta, Lord Nelson being seasick, Queen Victoria not being amused.

God has given us a sort of time machine, or, if you like, a collection of video tapes of various events in history – 'HIS . . . story' in the Old Testament. This collection of readings will take you through the Old Testament story in three months, a couple of chapters a day.

● Read each passage through as you would read any other book.

● Have a map of Israel and the Near East handy and follow the movement.

● Look up the things you don't understand in a Bible dictionary or handbook.

● Don't give up!

The beginning

Genesis	1–2	☐
	3–4	☐
	5–6	☐
	7–8	☐
Psalm	8	☐

Abraham

Genesis	12–13	☐
	14–15	☐
	16–17	☐
	18–19	☐
	20–21:7	☐

Joseph

Genesis	37–38	☐
	39–40	☐
	41–42	☐
	43–44	☐
	45–46	☐

Moses

Exodus	1–2	☐
	3–4	☐
	5–6	☐
	7–8	☐
	9–10	☐
	11–12	☐
	13–14	☐
	15–16	☐
	17–18	☐
	19–20	☐

Moses dies outside the promised land and Joshua is his successor.

Joshua and the invasion of Canaan

Joshua	1–2	☐
	3–4	☐
	5–6	☐
Psalm	1	☐
	20	☐
	23	☐
Joshua	7–8	☐
	9–10	☐
	11	☐

Early life in the promised land

a) Gideon – God's freedom fighter
Judges	6–8	☐

b) Samson – 'What a waste!'
Judges	13–14	☐
	15–16	☐

Israel becomes a kingdom

1 Samuel	8–9	☐
	10–11	☐
	12–13	☐
	14–15	☐

David, the shepherd king

1 Samuel	16–18	☐
2 Samuel	1–2	☐
	3–4	☐
	5–6	☐
	7–8	☐
	9–10	☐
	11–12	☐

(See Psalm 51 also)

Solomon

1 Kings	1–2	☐
	3–4	☐
	5–6	☐
	7–8	☐
	9–10	☐
	11	☐

(See Proverbs 1 also)

Civil War! . . . almost

1 Kings	12	☐

After this division, the Bible tells the sordid tale of increasingly godless leadership, disobedience, spreading paganism and injustice. During this phase of history, God sent many prophets, such as Isaiah and Micah, to warn the disobedient that God would punish them, and to encourage the faithful that the great Saviour or 'Messiah' would one day come. Spot the Messiah in the next passages.

Micah	1–2	☐
	3–4	☐
	5–6	☐
	7	☐
Habbakuk	1	☐
	2	☐
	3	☐

The warnings were ignored. God's judgments on Israel and Judah were devastating:

2 Kings	15–17	☐
	24–25	☐
Lamentations	1	☐
Psalm	137	☐

But God never really gives up. To see how he worked during the Exile, we follow the fortunes of two aristocratic Jews who escaped the horrors of forced labour: Daniel and Esther.

Daniel

Daniel	1–2	☐
	3–4	☐
	5–6	☐

Esther

– she saves the Jews from annihilation by winning a beauty competition!

Esther	1–2	☐
	3–4	☐
	5–6	☐
	7–8	☐
	9–10	☐

The return from exile

Ezra rebuilds the temple

Ezra	1	☐
	3–4	☐
	5–6	☐
	7–8	☐
	9–10	☐

Nehemiah rebuilds a city

Nehemiah	1–2	☐
	3–4	☐
	5–6	☐
	7–8	☐
	9–10	☐
	11–13	☐

How great is our God!

Psalms	90–91	☐
	92–93	☐
	94–95	☐
	96–97	☐
	98–99	☐

The day of the Lord

| Malachi | 1–2 | ☐ |
| | 3–4 | ☐ |

What the books are about

*T*HE books of the Old Testament are not arranged in chronological order, but grouped together according to literary style. So historical records, poetry, prophecies, or ritual rules are put together. This brief explanation of each book will help you get the gist of it before you read it.

Genesis
The creation of life, the universe and everything, and the origin of humanity's rebellion against God. With Noah and Abraham, God begins to pick up the pieces and save humankind.

Exodus
The escape of Israel from slavery in Egypt, and how God brings them into a new relationship with himself.

Leviticus
Laws about sacrifices and purity to demonstrate that God is holy and expects his people to be holy too.

Numbers
More laws, and the story of the Israelites wandering in the Sinai peninsula.

Deuteronomy
Final instructions to the people before they enter the promised land.

Joshua
The invasion and settlement of Canaan.

Judges
Contains a resumé of the conquest of Canaan from another angle, plus the biographies of people called Judges who ruled Israel on God's behalf.

Ruth
The story of a foreign girl who finds a new home among God's people.

1 and 2 Samuel
In the Hebrew Bible this is one book, not two. It describes the struggle against the Philistines, and the emergence of the first Hebrew kings, Saul and David.

1 and 2 Kings
Describes the reign of Solomon and how the kingdoms of Israel and Judah divided. The subsequent history of Israel and Judah is told.

1 and 2 Chronicles
The history of God's people from the death of Saul to the return from the Babylonian exile. These books repeat the story of 1 Samuel to 2 Kings but from a different angle.

Ezra and Nehemiah
Tell of the rebuilding of the city walls and temple in Jerusalem after the Exile, and how the Jews were made spiritually and militarily secure again.

Esther
The story of a Jewess who becomes a Persian queen and prevents the extermination of the Jews in Persia.

Job
A long discussion between Job and his friends on the reasons behind suffering.

Psalms
A collection of songs and poems for all occasions, written at various times during Israel's history.

Proverbs
A collection of wise sayings.

Ecclesiastes
Solomon's thoughts about the meaninglessness of life without God.

Song of Solomon
A poetic drama about the love between a man and a woman.

Isaiah
A warning about the coming exile, and promises about the return, and the future Messiah.

Jeremiah
More warnings about the dangers of neglecting God's ways, and promises about the coming of the new covenant (chapter 13).

Lamentations
A song of mourning after the destruction of Jerusalem by the Babylonians.

Ezekiel
Visions and experiences of a Jewish labourer in Babylon.

Daniel
The biography of a Jewish prince in the Babylonian court and the visions God gave him.

Hosea
Prophecies of the man who was told by the Lord to marry an immoral woman as a visual aid of the people's desertion of God.

Joel
Prophecies concerning the more intimate relationship God will have with people when he pours out his Spirit.

Amos
The prophecies of a shepherd who spoke out against social injustice and oppression during a particularly prosperous period in Israel's history.

Obadiah
How God will punish the land of Edom.

Jonah
The story of a prophet who tried to avoid God's call, and what happened when he eventually obeyed.

Micah
Tells of God's impending judgment on Judah.

Nahum
Describes how God will punish disobedient nations.

Habakkuk

A man's conversations with God about the coming of the Babylonian invaders, and the problem of evil.

Zephaniah

God's judgment of Israel and other nations, and the restoration of his people's glory.

Haggai

Set in the depressed years after the return from exile, when drought and poverty demoralize the people, Haggai encouraged them to keep on with the work of rebuilding the temple.

Zechariah

Visions and prophecies calling God's children to repentance, and promising the future restoration of his people.

Malachi

A call to holiness and obedience, with the promise that God will come in judgment and restoration.